THE RAGE OF ACHILLES

HOMER

THE RAGE OF ACHILLES FROM THE ILIAD

TRANSLATED BY ROBERT FAGLES
INTRODUCTION BY BERNARD KNOX

PENGUIN BOOKS

PENGUIN BOOKS

Published by the Penguin Group
Penguin Books USA Inc., 375 Hudson Street,
New York, New York 10014, U.S.A.
Penguin Books Ltd, 27 Wrights Lane, London W8 5TZ, England
Penguin Books Australia Ltd, Ringwood, Victoria, Australia
Penguin Books Canada Ltd, 10 Alcorn Avenue,
Toronto, Ontario, Canada M4V 3B2
Penguin Books (N.Z.) Ltd, 182–190 Wairau Road,
Auckland 10, New Zealand

Penguin Books Ltd, Registered Offices:
Harmondsworth, Middlesex, England

Published in Penguin Books 1995

These selections are from Robert Fagles's translation of *The Iliad*,
published by Penguin Books. Books 18 and 22 appeared origi-
nally in *Grand Street*.

ISBN 0 14 60.0196 6

Printed in the United States of America

Contents

Introduction

"Iliad" is a word that means "a poem about Ilium" (i.e., Troy), and Homer's great epic poem has been known as "The *Iliad*" ever since the Greek historian Herodotus so referred to it in the fifth century B.C. But the title is not an adequate description of the contents of the poem, which are best summed up in its opening line: "the rage of Peleus' son Achilles." The incident that provoked Achilles' rage took place in the tenth and final year of the Achaean attack on Troy, and though Homer does work into his narrative scenes that recall earlier stages of the war (the muster of the Achaean forces in Book 2, for example, and Priam's first sight of Agamemnon and the other Achaean chieftains in Book 3), the rage of Achilles—its cause, its course and its disastrous consequences—is the theme of the poem, the mainspring of the plot.

Chryses, a priest of Apollo, whose daughter has been carried off by the Achaeans in one of their raids, comes to the camp to ransom her. But she has been assigned, in the division of the booty, to the king who commands the Achaean army, Agamemnon, and he refuses to give her up. Her father prays for help to Apollo, who sends a plague that devastates the Achaean camp. Achilles, leader of the Myrmidons, one of the largest contingents of the Achaean army, summons the chieftains to an assembly. There they are told by the prophet Calchas that the girl must be returned to her father. Agamemnon has to give her up, but demands compensation for his loss. Achilles objects: let Agamemnon wait until more booty is taken. A violent quarrel breaks out between the two men, and Agamemnon finally announces that he will take recompense for his loss from Achilles, in the form of the girl Briseis, Achilles' share of the booty. Achilles represses an urge to kill Agamemnon and withdraws from the assembly, threatening to leave for home, with all his troops, the next day. The priest's daughter is restored to him, Apollo puts an end to the plague, and Briseis is taken away from Achilles' tent by Agamemnon's heralds.

Achilles turns to his goddess mother Thetis, asking her to prevail on Zeus, father of gods and men, to inflict loss and defeat on the Achaeans, so that they will realize how much they need him. Zeus is won over by Thetis (to whom he is indebted for help on a previous occasion), and in spite of the vehement objections of his wife Hera (who, like his daughter Athena, hates the Trojans and works for their destruction), he turns the tide of battle against the Achaeans. The Trojan leader Hector, son of Troy's old King Priam, drives the Achaeans back on their beached ships, round which they are forced to build a wall and ditch. At the urging of his chieftains, Agamemnon sends ambassadors to Achilles, offering him rich prizes and the hand of his daughter in marriage if he will return to the fighting line. The offer is refused, but the pleas of one of the ambassadors, Phoenix, an older man who belongs to Achilles' household, do have some effect: Achilles withdraws his threat to leave the next day; he will stay until Hector and the Trojans reach his own ships.

The battle resumes and now the Trojan onslaught breaches the wall and threatens the ships. The Achaean chieftains—Agamemnon, his brother Menelaus, Diomedes and Odysseus—are wounded one by one. Achilles' closest friend, Patroclus, sent by Achilles to find out how things stand in the Achaean camp, brings back the news and also pleads with Achilles to relent. He does so only partly; he agrees to let Patroclus go into battle with Achilles' troops, wearing Achilles' armor. This is enough: the Trojans in their turn are thrown back. But Patroclus is killed by the god Apollo, Troy's protector, and by Hector, who strips off Achilles' armor and puts it on himself.

Achilles' rage is now directed against Hector, the killer of his dearest friend. He is reconciled with Agamemnon, and as soon as his mother brings him a splendid suit of armor, made by the smith-god Hephaestus, he returns to the battle, and after slaughtering many Trojans, meets and kills Hector. He lashes Hector's corpse to his chariot and drags it to his own tent; he intends to throw it to the dogs and birds of prey. For Patroclus he holds a magnificent funeral, complete with athletic contests and human sacrifice. Whenever renewed grief for the loss of his friend overcomes him, he drags Hector's body around Patroclus' grave. But the body has been preserved from corruption by divine intervention, and the gods now decide (not unanimously for Hera and Athena object) to send a message to Achilles through his mother: he is to release Hector's body for ransom paid by King Priam of Troy. Achilles agrees, but what he does not anticipate is the arrival in his tent of Priam himself, alone, in the middle of the night. Instead of sending a herald, he has brought the ransom himself and begs for the body of his son. Achilles is reminded of his own father, also an old man who will never see his son again; Achilles knows, for his mother has told him, that his death is to come soon after Hector's. He sends Priam safely back with Hector's body to Troy and so, runs the last line of the poem, "the Trojans buried Hector breaker of horses" (24.944 in the translation). We know already that the death of Troy's main defender seals the fate of the city and that, as Thetis told Achilles: "hard on the heels of Hector's death your death must come at once" (18.112–13).

This summary is the bare bones of an epic poem that consists in the original Greek of 15,693 lines of hexameter verse, composed—probably in the late eighth or early seventh century B.C.—by a poet known to later ages as Homer, for whose life and activity no trustworthy information has come down to us. The poem, in other words, is some 2,700 years old.

Book One
The Rage of Achilles

Rage—Goddess, sing the rage of Peleus' son Achilles,
murderous, doomed, that cost the Achaeans countless losses,
hurling down to the House of Death so many sturdy souls,
great fighters' souls, but made their bodies carrion,
feasts for the dogs and birds,
and the will of Zeus was moving toward its end.
Begin, Muse, when the two first broke and clashed,
Agamemnon lord of men and brilliant Achilles.

What god drove them to fight with such a fury?
Apollo the son of Zeus and Leto. Incensed at the king
he swept a fatal plague through the army—men were dying
and all because Agamemnon spurned Apollo's priest.
Yes, Chryses approached the Achaeans' fast ships
to win his daughter back, bringing a priceless ransom
and bearing high in hand, wound on a golden staff,
the wreaths of the god, the distant deadly Archer.
He begged the whole Achaean army but most of all
the two supreme commanders, Atreus' two sons,
"Agamemnon, Menelaus—all Argives geared for war!
May the gods who hold the halls of Olympus give you
Priam's city to plunder, then safe passage home.

Just set my daughter free, my dear one . . . here,
accept these gifts, this ransom. Honor the god
who strikes from worlds away—the son of Zeus, Apollo!"

And all ranks of Achaeans cried out their assent:
"Respect the priest, accept the shining ransom!"
But it brought no joy to the heart of Agamemnon.
The king dismissed the priest with a brutal order
ringing in his ears: "Never again, old man,
let me catch sight of you by the hollow ships!
Not loitering now, not slinking back tomorrow.
The staff and the wreaths of god will never save you then,
The girl—I won't give up the girl. Long before that,
old age will overtake her in *my* house, in Argos,
far from her fatherland, slaving back and forth
at the loom, forced to share my bed!

                                        Now go,
don't tempt my wrath—and you may depart alive."

The old man was terrified. He obeyed the order,
turning, trailing away in silence down the shore
where the roaring battle lines of breakers crash and drag.
And moving off to a safe distance, over and over
the old priest prayed to the son of sleek-haired Leto,
lord Apollo, "Hear me, Apollo! God of the silver bow
who strides the walls of Chryse and Cilla sacrosanct—
lord in power of Tenedos—Smintheus, god of the plague!
If I ever roofed a shrine to please your heart,

2

ever burned the long rich bones of bulls and goats
on your holy altar, now, now bring my prayer to pass.
Pay the Danaans back—your arrows for my tears!"

His prayer went up and Phoebus Apollo heard him.
Down he strode from Olympus' peaks, storming at heart
with his bow and hooded quiver slung across his shoulders.
The arrows clanged at his back as the god quaked with rage,
the god himself on the march and down he came like night.
Over against the ships he dropped to a knee, let fly a shaft
and a terrifying clash rang out from the great silver bow.
First he went for the mules and circling dogs but then,
launching a piercing shaft at the men themselves,
he cut them down in droves—
and the corpse-fires burned on, night and day, no end in
    sight.

Nine days the arrows of god swept through the army.
On the tenth Achilles called all ranks to muster—
the impulse seized him, sent by white-armed Hera
grieving to see Achaean fighters drop and die.
Once they'd gathered, crowding the meeting grounds,
the swift runner Achilles rose and spoke among them:
"Son of Atreus, now we are beaten back, I fear,
the long campaign is lost. So home we sail . . .
if we can escape our death—if war and plague
are joining forces now to crush the Argives.
But wait: let us question a holy man,

3

a prophet, even a man skilled with dreams—
dreams as well can come our way from Zeus—
come, someone to tell us why Apollo rages so,
whether he blames us for a vow we failed, or sacrifice.
If only the god would share the smoky savor of lambs
and full-grown goats, Apollo might be willing, still,
somehow, to save us from this plague."

So he proposed
and down he sat again as Calchas rose among them,
Thestor's son, the clearest by far of all the seers
who scan the flight of birds. He knew all things that are,
all things that are past and all that are to come,
the seer who had led the Argive ships to Troy
with the second sight that god Apollo gave him.
For the armies' good the seer began to speak:
"Achilles, dear to Zeus . . .
you order me to explain Apollo's anger,
the distant deadly Archer? I will tell it all.
But strike a pact with me, swear you will defend me
with all your heart, with words and strength of hand.
For there is a man I will enrage—I see it now—
a powerful man who lords it over all the Argives,
one the Achaeans must obey . . . A mighty king,
raging against an inferior, is too strong.
Even if he can swallow down his wrath today,
still he will nurse the burning in his chest
until, sooner or later, he sends it bursting forth.
Consider it closely, Achilles. Will you save me?"

And the matchless runner reassured him: "Courage!
Out with it now, Calchas. Reveal the will of god,
whatever you may know. And I swear by Apollo
dear to Zeus, the power you pray to, Calchas,
when you reveal god's will to the Argives—no one,
not while I am alive and see the light on earth, no one
will lay his heavy hands on you by the hollow ships.
None among all the armies. Not even if you mean
Agamemnon here who now claims to be, by far,
the best of the Achaeans."

The seer took heart
and this time he spoke out, bravely: "Beware—
he casts no blame for a vow we failed, a sacrifice.
The god's enraged because Agamemnon spurned his priest,
he refused to free his daughter, he refused the ransom.
That's why the Archer sends us pains and he will send us
      more
and never drive this shameful destruction from the Argives,
not till we give back the girl with sparkling eyes
to her loving father—no price, no ransom paid—
and carry a sacred hundred bulls to Chryse town.
Then we can calm the god, and only then appease him."

So he declared and sat down. But among them rose
the fighting son of Atreus, lord of the far-flung kingdoms,
Agamemnon—furious, his dark heart filled to the brim,
blazing with anger now, his eyes like searing fire.
With a sudden, killing look he wheeled on Calchas first:

"Seer of misery! Never a word that works to my advantage!
Always misery warms your heart, your prophecies—
never a word of profit said or brought to pass.
Now, again, you divine god's will for the armies,
bruit it about, as fact, why the deadly Archer
multiplies our pains: because I, I refused
that glittering price for the young girl Chryseis.
Indeed, I prefer *her* by far, the girl herself,
I want her mine in my own house! I rank her higher
than Clytemnestra, my wedded wife—she's nothing less
in build or breeding, in mind or works of hand.
But I am willing to give her back, even so,
if that is best for all. What I really want
is to keep my people safe, not see them dying.
But fetch me another prize, and straight off too,
else I alone of the Argives go without my honor.
That would be a disgrace. You are all witness,
look—*my* prize is snatched away!"

> But the swift runner
Achilles answered him at once, "Just how, Agamemnon,
great field marshal . . . most grasping man alive,
how can the generous Argives give you prizes now?
I know of no troves of treasure, piled, lying idle,
anywhere. Whatever we dragged from towns we plundered,
all's been portioned out. But collect it, call it back
from the rank and file? *That* would be the disgrace.
So return the girl to the god, at least for now.
We Achaeans will pay you back, three, four times over,

6

if Zeus will grant us the gift, somehow, someday,
to raze Troy's massive ramparts to the ground."

But King Agamemnon countered, "Not so quickly,
brave as you are, godlike Achilles—trying to cheat *me*.
Oh no, you won't get past me, take me in that way!
What do you want? To cling to your own prize
while I sit calmly by—empty-handed here?
Is that why you order me to give her back?
No—if our generous Argives *will* give me a prize,
a match for my desires, equal to what I've lost,
well and good. But if they give me nothing
I will take a prize myself—your own, or Ajax'
or Odysseus' prize—I'll commandeer her myself
and let that man I go to visit choke with rage!
Enough. We'll deal with all this later, in due time.
Now come, we haul a black ship down to the bright sea,
gather a decent number of oarsmen along her locks
and put aboard a sacrifice, and Chryseis herself,
in all her beauty . . . we embark her too.
Let one of the leading captains take command.
Ajax, Idomeneus, trusty Odysseus or you, Achilles,
you—the most violent man alive—so you can perform
the rites for us and calm the god yourself."

                                        A dark glance
and the headstrong runner answered him in kind: "Shame-
    less—
armored in shamelessness—always shrewd with greed!

How could any Argive soldier obey your orders,
freely and gladly do your sailing for you
or fight your enemies, full force? Not I, no.
It wasn't Trojan spearmen who brought me here to fight.
The Trojans never did *me* damage, not in the least,
they never stole my cattle or my horses, never
in Phthia where the rich soil breeds strong men
did they lay waste my crops. How could they?
Look at the endless miles that lie between us . . .
shadowy mountain ranges, seas that surge and thunder.
No, you colossal, shameless—we all followed you,
to please you, to fight for you, to win your honor
back from the Trojans—Menelaus and you, you dog-face!
What do *you* care? Nothing. You don't look right or left.
And now you threaten to strip me of my prize in person—
the one I fought for long and hard, and sons of Achaea
handed her to me.

        My honors never equal yours,
whenever we sack some wealthy Trojan stronghold—
my arms bear the brunt of the raw, savage fighting,
true, but when it comes to dividing up the plunder
the lion's share is yours, and back I go to my ships,
clutching some scrap, some pittance that I love,
when I have fought to exhaustion.

        No more now—
back I go to Phthia. Better that way by far,
to journey home in the beaked ships of war.

I have no mind to linger here disgraced,
brimming your cup and piling up your plunder."

But the lord of men Agamemnon shot back,
"*Desert*, by all means—if the spirit drives you home!
I will never beg you to stay, not on *my* account.
Never—others will take my side and do me honor,
Zeus above all, whose wisdom rules the world.
You—I hate you most of all the warlords
loved by the gods. Always dear to your heart,
strife, yes, and battles, the bloody grind of war.
What if you are a great soldier? That's just a gift of god.
Go home with your ships and comrades, lord it over
     your Myrmidons!
You *are* nothing to me—you and your overweening anger!
But let this be my warning on your way:
since Apollo insists on taking my Chryseis,
I'll send her back in my own ships with *my* crew.
But I, I will be there in person at your tents
to take Briseis in all her beauty, your own prize—
so you can learn just how much greater I am than you
and the next man up may shrink from matching words with
     me,
from hoping to rival Agamemnon strength for strength!"

He broke off and anguish gripped Achilles.
The heart in his rugged chest was pounding, torn . . .
Should he draw the long sharp sword slung at his hip,

thrust through the ranks and kill Agamemnon now?—
or check his rage and beat his fury down?
As his racing spirit veered back and forth,
just as he drew his huge blade from its sheath,
down from the vaulting heavens swept Athena,
the white-armed goddess Hera sped her down:
Hera loved both men and cared for both alike.
Rearing behind him Pallas seized his fiery hair—
only Achilles saw her, none of the other fighters—
struck with wonder he spun around, he knew her at once,
Pallas Athena! the terrible blazing of those eyes,
and his winged words went flying: "Why, why now?
Child of Zeus with the shield of thunder, why come now?
To witness the outrage Agamemnon just committed?
I tell you this, and so help me it's the truth—
he'll soon pay for his arrogance with his life!"

Her gray eyes clear, the goddess Athena answered,
"Down from the skies I come to check your rage
if only you will yield.
The white-armed goddess Hera sped me down:
she loves you both, she cares for you both alike.
Stop this fighting, now. Don't lay hand to sword.
Lash him with threats of the price that he will face.
And I tell you this—and I *know* it is the truth—
one day glittering gifts will lie before you,
three times over to pay for all his outrage.
Hold back now. Obey us both."

So she urged
and the swift runner complied at once: "I must—
when the two of you hand down commands, Goddess,
a man submits though his heart breaks with fury.
Better for him by far. If a man obeys the gods
they're quick to hear his prayers."

                              And with that
Achilles stayed his burly hand on the silver hilt
and slid the huge blade back in its sheath.
He would not fight the orders of Athena.
Soaring home to Olympus, she rejoined the gods
aloft in the halls of Zeus whose shield is thunder.

But Achilles rounded on Agamemnon once again,
lashing out at him, not relaxing his anger for a moment:
"Staggering drunk, with your dog's eyes, your fawn's heart!
Never once did you arm with the troops and go to battle
or risk an ambush packed with Achaea's picked men—
you lack the courage, you can see death coming.
Safer by far, you find, to foray all through camp,
commandeering the prize of any man who speaks against
    you.
King who devours his people! Worthless husks, the men you
    rule—
if not, Atrides, this outrage would have been your last.
I tell you this, and I swear a mighty oath upon it . . .
by this, this scepter, look,
that never again will put forth crown and branches,

11

now it's left its stump on the mountain ridge forever,
nor will it sprout new green again, now the brazen ax
has stripped its bark and leaves, and now the sons of Achaea
pass it back and forth as they hand their judgments down,
upholding the honored customs whenever Zeus commands—
This scepter will be the mighty force behind my oath:
someday, I swear, a yearning for Achilles will strike
Achaea's sons and all your armies! But then, Atrides,
harrowed as you will be, *nothing* you do can save you—
not when your hordes of fighters drop and die,
cut down by the hands of man-killing Hector! Then—
then you will tear your heart out, desperate, raging
that you disgraced the best of the Achaeans!"

                                     Down on the ground
he dashed the scepter studded bright with golden nails,
then took his seat again. The son of Atreus smoldered,
glaring across at him, but Nestor rose between them,
the man of winning words, the clear speaker of Pylos . . .
Sweeter than honey from his tongue the voice flowed on and
    on.
Two generations of mortal men he had seen go down by
    now,
those who were born and bred with him in the old days,
in Pylos' holy realm, and now he ruled the third.
He pleaded with both kings, with clear good will,
"No more—or enormous sorrow comes to all Achaea!
How they would exult, Priam and Priam's sons
and all the Trojans. Oh they'd leap for joy

to hear the two of you battling on this way,
you who excel us all, first in Achaean councils,
first in the ways of war.
                              Stop. Please.
Listen to Nestor. You are both younger than I,
and in my time I struck up with better men than you,
even you, but never once did they make light of me.
I've never seen such men, I never will again . . .
men like Pirithous, Dryas, that fine captain,
Caeneus and Exadius, and Polyphemus, royal prince,
and Theseus, Aegeus' boy, a match for the immortals.
They were the strongest mortals ever bred on earth,
the strongest, and they fought against the strongest too,
shaggy Centaurs, wild brutes of the mountains—
they hacked them down, terrible, deadly work.
And I was in their ranks, fresh out of Pylos,
far away from home—they enlisted me themselves
and I fought on my own, a free lance, single-handed.
And none of the men who walk the earth these days
could battle with those fighters, none, but they,
they took to heart my counsels, marked my words.
So now you listen too. Yielding is far better . . .
Don't seize the girl, Agamemnon, powerful as you are—
leave her, just as the sons of Achaea gave her,
his prize from the very first.
And you, Achilles, never hope to fight it out
with your king, pitting force against his force:
no one can match the honors dealt a king, you know,

a sceptered king to whom great Zeus gives glory.
Strong as you are—a goddess was your mother—
he has more power because he rules more men.
Atrides, end your anger—look, it's Nestor!
I beg you, cool your fury against Achilles.
Here the man stands over all Achaea's armies,
our rugged bulwark braced for shocks of war."

But King Agamemnon answered him in haste,
"True, old man—all you say is fit and proper—
but this soldier wants to tower over the armies,
he wants to rule over all, to lord it over all,
give out orders to every man in sight. Well,
there's one, I trust, who will never yield to him!
What if the everlasting gods have made a spearman of him?
Have they entitled him to hurl abuse at *me*?"

"Yes!"—blazing Achilles broke in quickly—
"What a worthless, burnt-out coward I'd be called
if I would submit to you and all your orders,
whatever you blurt out. Fling them at others,
don't give me commands!
Never again, *I* trust, will Achilles yield to *you*.
And I tell you this—take it to heart, I warn you—
my hands will never do battle for that girl,
neither with you, King, nor any man alive.
You Achaeans gave her, now you've snatched her back.
But all the rest I possess beside my fast black ship—

not one bit of it can you seize against my will, Atrides.
Come, try it! So the men can see, that instant,
your black blood gush and spurt around my spear!"

Once the two had fought it out with words,
battling face-to-face, both sprang to their feet
and broke up the muster beside the Argive squadrons.
Achilles strode off to his trim ships and shelters,
back to his friend Patroclus and their comrades.
Agamemnon had a vessel hauled down to the sea,
he picked out twenty oarsmen to man her locks,
put aboard the cattle for sacrifice to the god
and led Chryseis in all her beauty amidships.
Versatile Odysseus took the helm as captain.

                              All embarked,
the party launched out on the sea's foaming lanes
while the son of Atreus told his troops to wash,
to purify themselves from the filth of plague.
They scoured it off, threw scourings in the surf
and sacrificed to Apollo full-grown bulls and goats
along the beaten shore of the fallow barren sea
and savory smoke went swirling up the skies.

So the men were engaged throughout the camp.
But King Agamemnon would not stop the quarrel,
the first threat he hurled against Achilles.
He called Talthybius and Eurybates briskly,

his two heralds, ready, willing aides:
"Go to Achilles' lodge. Take Briseis at once,
his beauty Briseis by the hand and bring her here.
But if he will not surrender her, I'll go myself,
I'll seize her myself, with an army at my back—
and all the worse for him!"

                He sent them off
with the strict order ringing in their ears.
Against their will the two men made their way
along the breaking surf of the barren salt sea
and reached the Myrmidon shelters and their ships.
They found him beside his lodge and black hull,
seated grimly—and Achilles took no joy
when he saw the two approaching.
They were afraid, they held the king in awe
and stood there, silent. Not a word to Achilles,
not a question. But he sensed it all in his heart,
their fear, their charge, and broke the silence for them:
"Welcome, couriers! Good heralds of Zeus and men,
here, come closer. You have done nothing to me.
You are not to blame. No one but Agamemnon—
he is the one who sent you for Briseis.
Go, Patroclus, Prince, bring out the girl
and hand her to them so they can take her back.
But let them both bear witness to my loss . . .
in the face of blissful gods and mortal men,
in the face of that unbending, ruthless king—
if the day should come when the armies need *me*

16

to save their ranks from ignominious, stark defeat.
The man is raving—with all the murderous fury in his heart.
He lacks the sense to see a day behind, a day ahead,
and safeguard the Achaeans battling by the ships."

Patroclus obeyed his great friend's command.
He led Briseis in all her beauty from the lodge
and handed her over to the men to take away.
And the two walked back along the Argive ships
while she trailed on behind, reluctant, every step.
But Achilles wept, and slipping away from his companions,
far apart, sat down on the beach of the heaving gray sea
and scanned the endless ocean. Reaching out his arms,
again and again he prayed to his dear mother: "Mother!
You gave me life, short as that life will be,
so at least Olympian Zeus, thundering up on high,
should give me honor—but now he gives me nothing.
Atreus' son Agamemnon, for all his far-flung kingdoms—
the man disgraces me, seizes and keeps my prize,
he tears her away himself!"

So he wept and prayed
and his noble mother heard him, seated near her father,
the Old Man of the Sea in the salt green depths.
Suddenly up she rose from the churning surf
like mist and settling down beside him as he wept,
stroked Achilles gently, whispering his name, "My child—
why in tears? What sorrow has touched your heart?
Tell me, please. Don't harbor it deep inside you.

We must share it all."
                                    And now from his depths
the proud runner groaned: "You know, you know,
why labor through it all? You know it all so well . . .
We raided Thebe once, Eetion's sacred citadel,
we ravaged the place, hauled all the plunder here
and the armies passed it round, share and share alike,
and they chose the beauty Chryseis for Agamemnon.
But soon her father, the holy priest of Apollo
the distant deadly Archer, Chryses approached
the fast trim ships of the Argives armed in bronze
to win his daughter back, bringing a priceless ransom
and bearing high in hand, wound on a golden staff,
the wreaths of the god who strikes from worlds away.
He begged the whole Achaean army but most of all
the two supreme commanders, Atreus' two sons,
and all ranks of Achaeans cried out their assent,
'Respect the priest, accept the shining ransom!'
But it brought no joy to the heart of Agamemnon,
our high and mighty king dismissed the priest
with a brutal order ringing in his ears.
And shattered with anger, the old man withdrew
but Apollo heard his prayer—he loved him, deeply—
he loosed his shaft at the Argives, withering plague,
and now the troops began to drop and die in droves,
the arrows of god went showering left and right,
whipping through the Achaeans' vast encampment.
But the old seer who knew the cause full well

revealed the will of the archer god Apollo.
And I was the first, mother, I urged them all,
'Appease the god at once!' That's when the fury
gripped the son of Atreus. Agamemnon leapt to his feet
and hurled his threat—his threat's been driven home.
One girl, Chryseis, the fiery-eyed Achaeans
ferry out in a fast trim ship to Chryse Island,
laden with presents for the god. The other girl,
just now the heralds came and led her away from camp,
Briseus' daughter, the prize the armies gave me.
But you, mother, if you have any power at all,
protect your son! Go to Olympus, plead with Zeus,
if you ever warmed his heart with a word or any action . . .

Time and again I heard your claims in father's halls,
boasting how you and you alone of all the immortals
rescued Zeus, the lord of the dark storm cloud,
from ignominious, stark defeat.
That day the Olympians tried to chain him down,
Hera, Poseidon lord of the sea, and Pallas Athena—
you rushed to Zeus, dear Goddess, broke those chains,
quickly ordered the hundred-hander to steep Olympus,
that monster whom the immortals call Briareus
but every mortal calls the Sea-god's son, Aegaeon,
though he's stronger than his father. Down he sat,
flanking Cronus' son, gargantuan in the glory of it all,
and the blessed gods were struck with terror then,
they stopped shackling Zeus.

Remind him of that,
now, go and sit beside him, grasp his knees . . .
persuade him, somehow, to help the Trojan cause,
to pin the Achaeans back against their ships,
trap them round the bay and mow them down.
So all can reap the benefits of their king—
so even mighty Atrides can see how mad he was
to disgrace Achilles, the best of the Achaeans!"

And Thetis answered, bursting into tears,
"O my son, my sorrow, why did I ever bear you?
All I bore was doom . . .
Would to god you could linger by your ships
without a grief in the world, without a torment!
Doomed to a short life, you have so little time.
And not only short, now, but filled with heartbreak too,
more than all other men alive—doomed twice over.
Ah to a cruel fate I bore you in our halls!
Still, I shall go to Olympus crowned with snow
and repeat your prayer to Zeus who loves the lightning.
Perhaps he will be persuaded.
But you, my child,
stay here by the fast ships, rage on at the Achaeans,
just keep clear of every foray in the fighting.
Only yesterday Zeus went off to the Ocean River
to feast with the Aethiopians, loyal, lordly men,
and all the gods went with him. But in twelve days
the Father returns to Olympus. Then, for your sake,

up I go to the bronze floor, the royal house of Zeus—
I'll grasp his knees, I think I'll win him over."

                                    With that vow
his mother went away and left him there, alone,
his heart inflamed for the sashed and lovely girl
they'd wrenched away from him against his will.
Meanwhile Odysseus drew in close to Chryse Island,
bearing the splendid sacrifice in the vessel's hold.
And once they had entered the harbor deep in bays
they furled and stowed their sails in the black ship,
they lowered the mast by the forestays, smoothly,
quickly let it down on the forked mast-crutch
and rowed her into a mooring under oars.
Out went the bow-stones—cables fast astern—
and the crew themselves climbed out in the breaking surf,
leading out the sacrifice for the archer god Apollo,
and out of the deep-sea ship Chryseis stepped too.
The tactful Odysseus led her up to the altar,
placing her in her loving father's arms, and said,
"Chryses, the lord of men Agamemnon sent me here
to bring your daughter back and perform a sacrifice,
a grand sacrifice to Apollo—for all Achaea's sake—
so we can appease the god
who's loosed such grief and torment on the Argives."

   With those words he left her in Chryses' arms
and the priest embraced the child he loved, exultant.
At once the men arranged the sacrifice for Apollo,

making the cattle ring his well-built altar,
then they rinsed their hands and took up barley.
Rising among them Chryses stretched his arms to the sky
and prayed in a high resounding voice, "Hear me, Apollo!
God of the silver bow who strides the walls of Chryse
and Cilla sacrosanct—lord in power of Tenedos!
If you honored me last time and heard my prayer
and rained destruction down on all Achaea's ranks,
now bring my prayer to pass once more. Now, at last,
drive this killing plague from the armies of Achaea!"

His prayer went up and Phoebus Apollo heard him.
And soon as the men had prayed and flung the barley,
first they lifted back the heads of the victims,
slit their throats, skinned them and carved away
the meat from the thighbones and wrapped them in fat,
a double fold sliced clean and topped with strips of flesh.
And the old man burned these on a dried cleft stick
and over the quarters poured out glistening wine
while young men at his side held five-pronged forks.
Once they had charred the thighs and tasted the organs
they cut the rest into pieces, pierced them with spits,
roasted them to a turn and pulled them off the fire.
The work done, the feast laid out, they ate well
and no man's hunger lacked a share of the banquet.
When they had put aside desire for food and drink,
the young men brimmed the mixing bowls with wine
and tipping first drops for the god in every cup
they poured full rounds for all. And all day long

they appeased the god with song, raising a ringing hymn
to the distant archer god who drives away the plague,
those young Achaean warriors singing out his power,
and Apollo listened, his great heart warm with joy.

Then when the sun went down and night came on
they made their beds and slept by the stern-cables . . .
When young Dawn with her rose-red fingers shone once
     more,
they set sail for the main encampment of Achaea.
The Archer sent them a bracing following wind,
they stepped the mast, spread white sails wide,
the wind hit full and the canvas bellied out
and a dark blue wave, foaming up at the bow,
sang out loud and strong as the ship made way,
skimming the whitecaps, cutting toward her goal.
And once offshore of Achaea's vast encampment
they eased her in and hauled the black ship high,
far up on the sand, and shored her up with timbers.
Then they scattered, each to his own ship and shelter.

But he raged on, grimly camped by his fast fleet,
the royal son of Peleus, the swift runner Achilles.
Now he no longer haunted the meeting grounds
where men win glory, now he no longer went to war
but day after day he ground his heart out, waiting there,
yearning, always yearning for battle cries and combat.

But now as the twelfth dawn after this shone clear
the gods who live forever marched home to Olympus,
all in a long cortege, and Zeus led them on.
And Thetis did not forget her son's appeals.
She broke from a cresting wave at first light
and soaring up to the broad sky and Mount Olympus,
found the son of Cronus gazing down on the world,
peaks apart from the other gods and seated high
on the topmost crown of rugged ridged Olympus.
And crouching down at his feet,
quickly grasping his knees with her left hand,
her right hand holding him underneath the chin,
she prayed to the lord god Zeus, the son of Cronus:
"Zeus, Father Zeus! If I ever served you well
among the deathless gods with a word or action,
bring this prayer to pass: honor my son Achilles!—
doomed to the shortest life of any man on earth.
And now the lord of men Agamemnon has disgraced him,
seizes and keeps his prize, tears her away himself. But you—
exalt him, Olympian Zeus: your urgings rule the world!
Come, grant the Trojans victory after victory
till the Achaean armies pay my dear son back,
building higher the honor he deserves!"

                              She paused
but Zeus who commands the storm clouds answered noth-
    ing.
The Father sat there, silent. It seemed an eternity . . .
but Thetis, clasping his knees, held on, clinging,

pressing her question once again: "Grant my prayer,
once and for all, Father, bow your head in assent!
Or deny me outright. What have you to fear?
So I may know, too well, just how cruelly
I am the most dishonored goddess of them all."

Filled with anger
Zeus who marshals the storm clouds answered her at last:
"Disaster. You will drive me into war with Hera.
She will provoke me, she with her shrill abuse.
Even now in the face of all the immortal gods
she harries me perpetually, Hera charges *me*
that I always go to battle for the Trojans.
Away with you now. Hera might catch us here.
I will see to this. I will bring it all to pass.
Look, I will bow my head if that will satisfy you.
That, I remind you, that among the immortal gods
is the strongest, truest sign that I can give.
No word or work of mine—nothing can be revoked,
there is no treachery, nothing left unfinished
once I bow my head to say it shall be done."

So he decreed. And Zeus the son of Cronus bowed
his craggy dark brows and the deathless locks came pouring
down from the thunderhead of the great immortal king
and giant shock waves spread through all Olympus.

So the two of them made their pact and parted.
Deep in the sea she dove from radiant Mount Olympus.

Zeus went back to his own halls, and all the gods
in full assembly rose from their seats at once
to meet the Father striding toward them now.
None dared remain at rest as Zeus advanced,
they all sprang up to greet him face-to-face
as he took his place before them on his throne.
But Hera knew it all. She had seen how Thetis,
the Old Man of the Sea's daughter, Thetis quick
on her glistening feet was hatching plans with Zeus.
And suddenly Hera taunted the Father, son of Cronus:
"So, who of the gods this time, my treacherous one,
was hatching plans with you?
Always your pleasure, whenever my back is turned,
to settle things in your grand clandestine way.
You never deign, do you, freely and frankly,
to share your plots with me—never, not a word!"

  The father of men and gods replied sharply,
"Hera—stop hoping to fathom all my thoughts.
You will find them a trial, though you are my wife.
Whatever is right for you to hear, no one, trust me,
will know of it before you, neither god nor man.
Whatever I choose to plan apart from all the gods—
no more of your everlasting questions, probe and pry no
    more."

  And Hera the Queen, her dark eyes wide, exclaimed,
"Dread majesty, son of Cronus, what are you saying?

26

Now surely I've never probed or pried in the past.
Why, you can scheme to your heart's content
without a qualm in the world for me. But now
I have a terrible fear that she has won you over,
Thetis, the Old Man of the Sea's daughter, Thetis
with her glistening feet. I know it. Just at dawn
she knelt down beside you and grasped your knees
and I suspect you bowed your head in assent to her—
you granted once and for all to exalt Achilles now
and slaughter hordes of Achaeans pinned against their
    ships."

     And Zeus who marshals the thunderheads returned,
"Maddening one . . . you and your eternal suspicions—
I can never escape you. Ah but tell me, Hera,
just what can you *do* about all this? Nothing.
Only estrange yourself from me a little more—
and all the worse for you.
If what you say is true, that must be my pleasure.
Now go sit down. Be quiet now. Obey my orders,
for fear the gods, however many Olympus holds,
are powerless to protect you when I come
to throttle you with my irresistible hands."

                                        He subsided
but Hera the Queen, her eyes wider, was terrified.
She sat in silence. She wrenched her will to his.

And throughout the halls of Zeus the gods of heaven
quaked with fear. Hephaestus the Master Craftsman
rose up first to harangue them all, trying now
to bring his loving mother a little comfort,
the white-armed goddess Hera: "Oh disaster . . .
that's what it is, and it will be unbearable
if the two of you must come to blows this way,
flinging the gods in chaos just for mortal men.
No more joy for us in the sumptuous feast
when riot rules the day.
I urge you, mother—you know that I am right—
work back into his good graces, so the Father,
our beloved Father will never wheel on us again,
send our banquets crashing! The Olympian lord of light-
    ning—
what if he would like to blast us from our seats?
He is far too strong. Go back to him, mother,
stroke the Father with soft, winning words—
at once the Olympian will turn kind to us again."

Pleading, springing up with a two-handled cup,
he reached it toward his loving mother's hands
with his own winning words: "Patience, mother!
Grieved as you are, bear up, or dear as you are,
I have to see you beaten right before my eyes.
I would be shattered—what could I do to save you?
It's hard to fight the Olympian strength for strength.

You remember the last time I rushed to your defense?
He seized my foot, he hurled me off the tremendous thresh-
    old
and all day long I dropped, I was dead weight and then,
when the sun went down, down I plunged on Lemnos,
little breath left in me. But the mortals there
soon nursed a fallen immortal back to life."

    At that the white-armed goddess Hera smiled
and smiling, took the cup from her child's hands.
Then dipping sweet nectar up from the mixing bowl
he poured it round to all the immortals, left to right.
And uncontrollable laughter broke from the happy gods
as they watched the god of fire breathing hard
and bustling through the halls.
                    That hour then
and all day long till the sun went down they feasted
and no god's hunger lacked a share of the handsome banquet
or the gorgeous lyre Apollo struck or the Muses singing
voice to voice in choirs, their vibrant music rising.

    At last, when the sun's fiery light had set,
each immortal went to rest in his own house,
the splendid high halls Hephaestus built for each
with all his craft and cunning, the famous crippled Smith.
And Olympian Zeus the lord of lightning went to his own
    bed

where he had always lain when welcome sleep came on him.
There he climbed and there he slept and by his side
lay Hera the Queen, the goddess of the golden throne.

. . .

Book Eighteen
The Shield of Achilles

So the men fought on like a mass of whirling fire
as swift Antilochus raced the message toward Achilles.
Sheltered under his curving, beaked ships he found him,
foreboding, deep down, all that had come to pass.
Agonizing now he probed his own great heart:
"Why, why? Our long-haired Achaeans routed again,
driven in terror off the plain to crowd the ships, but why?
Dear gods, don't bring to pass the grief that haunts my
       heart—
the prophecy that mother revealed to me one time . . .
she said the best of the Myrmidons—while I lived—
would fall at Trojan hands and leave the light of day.
And now he's dead, I know it. Menoetius' gallant son,
my headstrong friend! And I told Patroclus clearly,
'Once you have beaten off the lethal fire, quick,
come back to the ships—you must not battle Hector!' "

   As such fears went churning through his mind
the warlord Nestor's son drew near him now,
streaming warm tears, to give the dreaded message:
"Ah son of royal Peleus, what you must hear from me!
What painful news—would to god it had never happened!
Patroclus has fallen. They're fighting over his corpse.

He's stripped, naked—Hector with that flashing helmet,
Hector has your arms!"
                           So the captain reported,
A black cloud of grief came shrouding over Achilles.
Both hands clawing the ground for soot and filth,
he poured it over his head, fouled his handsome face
and black ashes settled onto his fresh clean war-shirt.
Overpowered in all his power, sprawled in the dust,
Achilles lay there, fallen . . .
tearing his hair, defiling it with his own hands.
And the women he and Patroclus carried off as captives
caught the grief in their hearts and keened and wailed,
out of the tents they ran to ring the great Achilles,
all of them beat their breasts with clenched fists,
sank to the ground, each woman's knees gave way.
Antilochus kneeling near, weeping uncontrollably,
clutched Achilles' hands as he wept his proud heart out—
for fear he would slash his throat with an iron blade.
Achilles suddenly loosed a terrible, wrenching cry
and his noble mother heard him, seated near her father,
the Old Man of the Sea in the salt green depths,
and she cried out in turn. And immortal sea-nymphs
gathered round their sister, all the Nereids dwelling
down the sounding depths, they all came rushing now—
Glitter, blossoming Spray and the swells' Embrace,
Fair-Isle and shadowy Cavern, Mist and Spindrift,
ocean nymphs of the glances pooling deep and dark,
Race-with-the-Waves and Headlands' Hope and Safe Haven,

Glimmer of Honey, Suave-and-Soothing, Whirlpool, Brilliance,
Bounty and First Light and Speeder of Ships and buoyant
  Power,
Welcome Home and Bather of Meadows and Master's Lovely
  Consort,
Gift of the Sea, Eyes of the World and the famous milk-white
  Calm
and Truth and Never-Wrong and the queen who rules the
  tides in beauty
and in rushed Glory and Healer of Men and the one who res-
  cues kings
and Sparkler, Down-from-the-Cliffs, sleek-haired Strands of
  Sand
and all the rest of the Nereids dwelling down the depths.
The silver cave was shimmering full of sea-nymphs,
all in one mounting chorus beating their breasts
as Thetis launched the dirge: "Hear me, sisters,
daughters of Nereus, so you all will know it well—
listen to all the sorrows welling in my heart!
I am agony—
                    mother of grief and greatness—O my child!
Yes, I gave birth to a flawless, mighty son . . .
the splendor of heroes, and he shot up like a young branch,
like a fine tree I reared him—the orchard's crowning glory—
but only to send him off in the beaked ships to Troy
to battle Trojans! Never again will I embrace him
striding home through the doors of Peleus' house.

And long as I have him with me, still alive,
looking into the sunlight, he is racked with anguish.
And I, I go to his side—nothing I do can help him.
Nothing. But go I shall, to see my darling boy,
to hear what grief has come to break his heart
while he holds back from battle."

So Thetis cried
as she left the cave and her sisters swam up with her,
all in a tide of tears, and billowing round them now
the ground swell heaved open. And once they reached
the fertile land of Troy they all streamed ashore,
row on row in a long cortege, the sea-nymphs
filing up where the Myrmidon ships lay hauled,
clustered closely round the great runner Achilles . . .
As he groaned from the depths his mother rose before him
and sobbing a sharp cry, cradled her son's head in her hands
and her words were all compassion, winging pity: "My
    child—
why in tears? What sorrow has touched your heart?
Tell me, please. Don't harbor it deep inside you.
Zeus has accomplished everything you wanted,
just as you raised your hands and prayed that day.
All the sons of Achaea are pinned against the ships
and all for want of you—they suffer shattering losses."

And groaning deeply the matchless runner answered,
"O dear mother, true! All those burning desires
Olympian Zeus has brought to pass for me—

but what joy to me now? My dear comrade's dead—
Patroclus—the man I loved beyond all other comrades,
loved as my own life—I've lost him—Hector's killed him,
stripped the gigantic armor off his back, a marvel to
    behold—
my burnished gear! Radiant gifts the gods presented Peleus
that day they drove you into a mortal's marriage bed . . .
I wish you'd lingered deep with the deathless sea-nymphs,
lived at ease, and Peleus carried home a mortal bride.
But now, as it is, sorrows, unending sorrows must surge
within your heart as well—for your own son's death.
Never again will you embrace him striding home.
My spirit rebels—I've lost the will to live,
to take my stand in the world of men—unless,
before all else, Hector's battered down by my spear
and gasps away his life, the blood-price for Patroclus,
Menoetius' gallant son he's killed and stripped!"

    But Thetis answered, warning through her tears,
"You're doomed to a short life, my son, from all you say!
For hard on the heels of Hector's death your death
must come at once—"

                    "Then let me die at once"—
Achilles burst out, despairing—"since it was not my fate
to save my dearest comrade from his death! Look,
a world away from his fatherland he's perished,
lacking me, my fighting strength, to defend him.
But now, since I shall not return to my fatherland . . .

nor did I bring one ray of hope to my Patroclus,
nor to the rest of all my steadfast comrades,
countless ranks struck down by mighty Hector—
No, no, here I sit by the ships . . .
a useless, dead weight on the good green earth—
I, no man my equal among the bronze-armed Achaeans,
not in battle, only in wars of words that others win.
If only strife could die from the lives of gods and men
and anger that drives the sanest man to flare in outrage—
bitter gall, sweeter than dripping streams of honey,
that swarms in people's chests and blinds like smoke—
just like the anger Agamemnon king of men
has roused within me now . . .
                              Enough.
Let bygones be bygones. Done is done.
Despite my anguish I will beat it down,
the fury mounting inside me, down by force.
But now I'll go and meet that murderer head-on,
that Hector who destroyed the dearest life I know.
For my own death, I'll meet it freely—whenever Zeus
and the other deathless gods would like to bring it on!
Not even Heracles fled his death, for all his power,
favorite son as he was to father Zeus the King.
Fate crushed him, and Hera's savage anger.
And I too, if the same fate waits for me . . .
I'll lie in peace, once I've gone down to death.
But now, for the moment, let me seize great glory!—
and drive some woman of Troy or deep-breasted Dardan

to claw with both hands at her tender cheeks and wipe away
her burning tears as the sobs come choking from her
   throat—
they'll learn that I refrained from war a good long time!
Don't try to hold me back from the fighting, mother,
love me as you do. You can't persuade me now."

   The goddess of the glistening feet replied,
"Yes, my son, you're right. No coward's work,
to save your exhausted friends from headlong death.
But your own handsome war-gear lies in Trojan hands,
bronze and burnished—and Hector in that flashing helmet,
Hector glories in your armor, strapped across his back.
Not that he will glory in it long, I tell you:
his own destruction hovers near him now. Wait—
don't fling yourself in the grind of battle yet,
not till you see me coming back with your own eyes.
Tomorrow I will return to you with the rising sun,
bearing splendid arms from Hephaestus, god of fire!"

   With that vow she turned away from her son
and faced and urged her sisters of the deep,
"Now down you go in the Ocean's folding gulfs
to visit father's halls—the Old Man of the Sea—
and tell him all. I am on my way to Olympus heights,
to the famous Smith Hephaestus—I pray he'll give my son
some fabulous armor full of the god's great fire!"

And under a foaming wave her sisters dove
as glistening-footed Thetis soared toward Olympus
to win her dear son an immortal set of arms.

                                        And now,
as her feet swept her toward Olympus, ranks of Achaeans,
fleeing man-killing Hector with grim, unearthly cries,
reached the ships and the Hellespont's long shore.
As for Patroclus, there seemed no hope that Achaeans
could drag the corpse of Achilles' comrade out of range.
Again the Trojan troops and teams overtook the body
with Hector son of Priam storming fierce as fire.
Three times illustrious Hector shouted for support,
seized his feet from behind, wild to drag him off,
three times the Aeantes, armored in battle-fury
fought him off the corpse. But Hector held firm,
staking all on his massive fighting strength—
again and again he'd hurl himself at the melee,
again and again stand fast with piercing cries
but he never gave ground backward, not one inch.
The helmed Aeantes could no more frighten Hector,
the proud son of Priam, back from Patroclus' corpse
than shepherds out in the field can scare a tawny lion
off his kill when the hunger drives the beast claw-mad.
And now Hector would have hauled the body away
and won undying glory . . .
if wind-swift Iris had not swept from Olympus
bearing her message—Peleus' son must arm—
but all unknown to Zeus and the other gods

since Hera spurred her on. Halting near
she gave Achilles a flight of marching orders:
"To arms—son of Peleus! Most terrifying man alive!
Defend Patroclus! It's all for him, this merciless battle
pitched before the ships. They're mauling each other now,
Achaeans struggling to save the corpse from harm,
Trojans charging to haul it back to windy Troy.
Flashing Hector's far in the lead, wild to drag it off,
furious to lop the head from its soft, tender neck
and stake it high on the city's palisade.

                      Up with you—
no more lying low! Writhe with shame at the thought
Patroclus may be sport for the dogs of Troy!
Yours, the shame will be yours
if your comrade's corpse goes down to the dead defiled!"

   But the swift runner replied, "Immortal Iris—
what god has sped you here to tell me this?"

   Quick as the wind the rushing Iris answered,
"Hera winged me on, the illustrious wife of Zeus.
But the son of Cronus throned on high knows nothing,
nor does any other immortal housed on Olympus
shrouded deep in snow."

                    Achilles broke in quickly—
"How can I go to war? The Trojans have my gear.
And my dear mother told me I must not arm for battle,
not till I see her coming back with my own eyes—

she vowed to bring me burnished arms from the god of fire.
I know of no other armor. Whose gear could I wear?
None but Telamonian Ajax' giant shield.
But he's at the front, I'm sure, engaging Trojans,
slashing his spear to save Patroclus' body."

Quick as the wind the goddess had a plan:
"We know—we too—they hold your famous armor.
Still, just as you are, go out to the broad trench
and show yourself to the Trojans. Struck with fear
at the sight of you, they might hold off from attack
and Achaea's fighting sons get second wind,
exhausted as they are . . .
Breathing room in war is all too brief."

And Iris racing the wind went veering off
as Achilles, Zeus's favorite fighter, rose up now
and over his powerful shoulder Pallas slung the shield,
the tremendous storm-shield with all its tassels flaring—
and crowning his head the goddess swept a golden cloud
and from it she lit a fire to blaze across the field.
As smoke goes towering up the sky from out a town
cut off on a distant island under siege . . .
enemies battling round it, defenders all day long
trading desperate blows from their own city walls
but soon as the sun goes down the signal fires flash,
rows of beacons blazing into the air to alert their
    neighbors—

if only they'll come in ships to save them from disaster—
so now from Achilles' head the blaze shot up the sky.
He strode from the rampart, took his stand at the trench
but he would not mix with the milling Argive ranks.
He stood in awe of his mother's strict command.
So there he rose and loosed an enormous cry
and off in the distance Pallas shrieked out too
and drove unearthly panic through the Trojans.
Piercing loud as the trumpet's battle cry that blasts
from murderous raiding armies ringed around some city—
so piercing now the cry that broke from Aeacides.
And Trojans hearing the brazen voice of Aeacides,
all their spirits quaked—even sleek-maned horses,
sensing death in the wind, slewed their chariots round
and charioteers were struck dumb when they saw that fire,
relentless, terrible, burst from proud-hearted Achilles' head,
blazing as fiery-eyed Athena fueled the flames. Three times
the brilliant Achilles gave his great war cry over the trench,
three times the Trojans and famous allies whirled in panic—
and twelve of their finest fighters died then and there,
crushed by chariots, impaled on their own spears.
And now the exultant Argives seized the chance
to drag Patroclus' body quickly out of range
and laid him on a litter . . .
Standing round him, loving comrades mourned,
and the swift runner Achilles joined them, grieving,
weeping warm tears when he saw his steadfast comrade
lying dead on the bier, mauled by tearing bronze,

the man he sent to war with team and chariot
but never welcomed home again alive.

Now Hera the ox-eyed queen of heaven drove the sun,
untired and all unwilling, to sink in the Ocean's depths
and the sun went down at last and brave Achaeans ceased
the grueling clash of arms, the leveling rout of war.

And the Trojans in turn, far across the field,
pulling forces back from the last rough assault,
freed their racing teams from under chariot yokes
but before they thought of supper, grouped for council.
They met on their feet. Not one of them dared to sit
for terror seized them all—the great Achilles
who held back from the brutal fighting so long
had just come blazing forth.
Panthous' son Polydamas led the debate,
a good clear head, and the only man who saw
what lay in the past and what the Trojans faced.
He was Hector's close comrade, born on the same night,
but excelled at trading words as he at trading spear-thrusts.
And now, with all good will, Polydamas rose and spoke:
"Weigh both sides of the crisis well, my friends.
What I urge is this: draw back to the city now.
Don't wait for the holy Dawn to find us here afield,
ranged by the ships—we're too far from our walls.
As long as that man kept raging at royal Agamemnon
the Argive troops were easier game to battle down.

I too was glad to camp the night on the shipways,
hopes soaring to seize their heavy rolling hulls.
But now racing Achilles makes my blood run cold.
So wild the man's fury he will never rest content,
holding out on the plain where Trojans and Argives
met halfway, exchanging blows in the savage onset—
never: *he* will fight for our wives, for Troy itself!
So retreat to Troy. Trust me—we will face disaster.
Now, for the moment, the bracing godsent night
has stopped the swift Achilles in his tracks.
But let him catch us lingering here tomorrow,
just as he rises up in arms—there may be some
who will sense his fighting spirit all too well.
You'll thank your stars to get back to sacred Troy,
whoever escapes him. Dogs and birds will have their fill—
of Trojan flesh, by heaven. Battalions of Trojans!
Pray god such grief will never reach my ears.
So follow my advice, hard as it may seem . . .
Tonight conserve our strength in the meeting place,
and the great walls and gates and timbered doors we hung,
well-planed, massive and bolted tight, will shield the city.
But tomorrow at daybreak, armed to the hilt for battle,
we man the towering ramparts. All the worse for him—
if Achilles wants to venture forth from the fleet,
fight us round our walls. Back to the ships he'll go,
once he's lashed the power out of his rippling stallions,
whipping them back and forth beneath our city walls.
Not even *his* fury will let him crash our gates—

he'll never plunder Troy.
Sooner the racing dogs will eat him raw!"

Helmet flashing, Hector wheeled with a dark glance:
"No more, Polydamas! Your pleading repels me now.
You say go back again—be crammed inside the city.
Aren't you sick of being caged inside those walls?
Time was when the world would talk of Priam's Troy
as the city rich in gold and rich in bronze—but now
our houses are stripped of all their sumptuous treasures,
troves sold off and shipped to Phrygia, lovely Maeonia,
once great Zeus grew angry . . .
But now, the moment the son of crooked Cronus
allows me to seize some glory here at the ships
and pin these Argives back against the sea—
you fool, enough! No more thoughts of retreat
paraded before our people. Not that one Trojan
will ever take your lead—I'll never permit it.
Come, follow my orders! All obey me now.
Take supper now. Take your posts through camp.
And no forgetting the watch, each man wide awake.
And any Trojan so weighed down, so oppressed
by his own possessions, let him collect the lot,
pass them round to the people—a grand public feast.
Far better for one of ours to reap the benefits
than all the marauding Argives. Then, as you say,
'tomorrow at daybreak, armed to the hilt for battle'—
we slash to attack against their deep curved hulls!

If it really *was* Achilles who reared beside the ships,
all the worse for him—if he wants his fill of war.
I for one, I'll never run from his grim assault,
I'll stand up to the man—see if he bears off glory
or I bear it off myself! The god of war is impartial:
he hands out death to the man who hands out death."

    So Hector finished. The Trojans roared assent,
lost in folly. Athena had swept away their senses.
They gave applause to Hector's ruinous tactics,
none to Polydamas, who gave them sound advice.
And now their entire army settled down to supper
but all night long the Argives raised Patroclus' dirge.
And Achilles led them now in a throbbing chant of sorrow,
laying his man-killing hands on his great friend's chest,
convulsed with bursts of grief. Like a bearded lion
whose pride of cubs a deer-hunter has snatched away,
out of some thick woods, and back he comes, too late,
and his heart breaks but he courses after the hunter,
hot on his tracks down glen on twisting glen—
where can he find him?—gripped by piercing rage . . .
so Achilles groaned, deeply, crying out to his Myrmidons,
"O my captains! How empty the promise I let fall
that day I reassured Menoetius in his house—
I promised the king I'd bring him back his son,
home to Opois, covered in glory, Troy sacked,
hauling his rightful share of plunder home, home.
But Zeus will never accomplish all our best-laid plans.

Look at us. Both doomed to stain red with our blood
the same plot of earth, a world away in Troy!
For not even *I* will voyage home again. Never.
No embrace in his halls from the old horseman Peleus
nor from mother, Thetis—this alien earth I stride
will hold me down at last.

                    But now, Patroclus,
since I will follow you underneath the ground,
I shall not bury you, no, not till I drag back here
the gear and head of Hector, who slaughtered you,
my friend, greathearted friend . . .
Here in front of your flaming pyre I'll cut the throats
of a dozen sons of Troy in all their shining glory,
venting my rage on them for your destruction!
Till then you lie as you are beside my beaked ships
and round you the Trojan women and deep-breasted Dar-
    dans
will mourn you night and day, weeping burning tears,
women we fought to win—strong hands and heavy lance—
whenever we sacked rich cities held by mortal men."

With that the brilliant Achilles ordered friends
to set a large three-legged cauldron over the fire
and wash the clotted blood from Patroclus' wounds
with all good speed. Hoisting over the blaze
a cauldron filled to the brim with bathing water,
they piled fresh logs beneath and lit them quickly.
The fire lapped at the vessel's belly, the water heated

and soon as it reached the boil in the glowing bronze
they bathed and anointed the body sleek with olive oil,
closed each wound with a soothing, seasoned unguent
and then they laid Patroclus on his bier . . .
covered him head to foot in a thin light sheet
and over his body spread the white linen shroud.
Then all night long, ringing the great runner Achilles,
Myrmidon fighters mourned and raised Patroclus' dirge.

But Zeus turned to Hera, his wife and sister, saying,
"So, my ox-eyed Queen, you've had your way at last,
setting the famous runner Achilles on his feet.
Mother Hera—look, these long-haired Achaeans
must be sprung of your own immortal loins."

But her eyes widening, noble Hera answered,
"Dread majesty, son of Cronus, what are you saying?
Even a mortal man will act to help a friend,
condemned as a mortal always is to death
and hardly endowed with wisdom deep as ours.
So how could I, claiming to be the highest goddess—
both by birth and since I am called your consort
and you in turn rule all the immortal gods—
how could I hold back from these, these Trojans,
men I loathe, and fail to weave their ruin?"

Now as the King and Queen provoked each other,
glistening-footed Thetis reached Hephaestus' house,

indestructible, bright as stars, shining among the gods,
built of bronze by the crippled Smith with his own hands.
There she found him, sweating, wheeling round his bellows,
pressing the work on twenty three-legged cauldrons,
an array to ring the walls inside his mansion.
He'd bolted golden wheels to the legs of each
so all on their own speed, at a nod from him,
they could roll to halls where the gods convene
then roll right home again—a marvel to behold.
But not quite finished yet . . .
the god had still to attach the inlaid handles.
These he was just fitting, beating in the rivets.
As he bent to the work with all his craft and cunning,
Thetis on her glistening feet drew near the Smith.
But Charis saw her first, Charis coming forward,
lithe and lovely in all her glittering headdress,
the Grace the illustrious crippled Smith had married.
Approaching Thetis, she caught her hand and spoke her
    name:
"Thetis of flowing robes! What brings you to our house?
A beloved, honored friend—but it's been so long,
your visits much too rare. Follow me in, please,
let me offer you all a guest could want."

                          Welcome words,
and the radiant goddess Charis led the way inside.
She seated her on a handsome, well-wrought chair,
studded with silver, under it slipped a stool
and called the famous Smith: "Hephaestus, come—

look who's here! Thetis would ask a favor of you!"

    And the famous crippled Smith exclaimed warmly,
"Thetis—here? Ah then a wondrous, honored goddess
comes to grace our house! Thetis saved my life
when the mortal pain came on me after my great fall,
thanks to my mother's will, that brazen bitch,
she wanted to hide me—because I was a cripple.
What shattering anguish I'd have suffered then
if Thetis had not taken me to her breast, Eurynome too,
the daughter of Ocean's stream that runs around the world.
Nine years I lived with both, forging bronze by the trove,
elegant brooches, whorled pins, necklaces, chokers, chains—
there in the vaulted cave—and round us Ocean's currents
swirled in a foaming, roaring rush that never died.
And no one knew. Not a single god or mortal,
only Thetis and Eurynome knew—they saved me.
And here is Thetis now, in our own house!
So I *must* do all I can to pay her back,
the price for the life she saved . . .
the nymph of the sea with sleek and lustrous locks.
Quickly, set before her stranger's generous fare
while I put away my bellows and all my tools."

                                        With that
he heaved up from the anvil block—his immense hulk
hobbling along but his shrunken legs moved nimbly.
He swung the bellows aside and off the fires,
gathered the tools he'd used to weld the cauldrons

49

and packed them all in a sturdy silver strongbox.
Then he sponged off his brow and both burly arms,
his massive neck and shaggy chest, pulled on a shirt
and grasping a heavy staff, Hephaestus left his forge
and hobbled on. Handmaids ran to attend their master,
all cast in gold but a match for living, breathing girls.
Intelligence fills their hearts, voice and strength their frames,
from the deathless gods they've learned their works of hand.
They rushed to support their lord as he went bustling on
and lurching nearer to Thetis, took his polished seat,
reached over to clutch her hand and spoke her name:
"Thetis of flowing robes! What brings you to our house?
A beloved, honored friend—but it's been so long,
your visits much too rare.
Tell me what's on your mind. I am eager to do it—
whatever I *can* do . . . whatever can be done."

But Thetis burst into tears, her voice welling:
"Oh Hephaestus—who of all the goddesses on Olympus,
who has borne such withering sorrows in her heart?
Such pain as Zeus has given me, above all others!
Me out of all the daughters of the sea he chose
to yoke to a mortal man, Peleus, son of Aeacus,
and I endured his bed, a mortal's bed, resisting
with all my will. And now he lies in the halls,
broken with grisly age, but now my griefs are worse.
Remember? Zeus also gave me a son to bear and breed,
the splendor of heroes, and he shot up like a young branch,

50

like a fine tree I reared him—the orchard's crowning glory—
but only to send him off in the beaked ships to Troy
to battle Trojans! Never again will I embrace him
striding home through the doors of Peleus' house.
And long as I have him with me, still alive,
looking into the sunlight, he is racked with anguish.
I go to his side—nothing I do can help him. Nothing.
That girl the sons of Achaea picked out for his prize—
right from his grasp the mighty Agamemnon tore her,
and grief for her has been gnawing at his heart.
But then the Trojans pinned the Achaeans tight
against their sterns, they gave them no way out,
and the Argive warlords begged my son to help,
they named in full the troves of glittering gifts
they'd send his way. But at that point he refused
to beat disaster off—refused himself, that is—
but he buckled his own armor round Patroclus,
sent him into battle with an army at his back.
And all day long they fought at the Scaean Gates,
that very day they would have stormed the city too,
if Apollo had not killed Menoetius' gallant son
as he laid the Trojans low—Apollo cut him down
among the champions there and handed Hector glory.
So now I come, I throw myself at your knees,
please help me! Give my son—he won't live long—
a shield and helmet and tooled greaves with ankle-straps
and armor for his chest. All that he had was lost,

lost when the Trojans killed his steadfast friend.
Now he lies on the ground—his heart is breaking."

And the famous crippled Smith replied, "Courage!
Anguish for all that armor—sweep it from your mind.
If only I could hide him away from pain and death,
that day his grim destiny comes to take Achilles,
as surely as glorious armor shall be his, armor
that any man in the world of men will marvel at
through all the years to come—whoever sees its splendor."

With that he left her there and made for his bellows,
turning them on the fire, commanding, "Work—to work!"
And the bellows, all twenty, blew on the crucibles,
breathing with all degrees of shooting, fiery heat
as the god hurried on—a blast for the heavy work,
a quick breath for the light, all precisely gauged
to the god of fire's wish and the pace of the work in hand.
Bronze he flung in the blaze, tough, durable bronze
and tin and priceless gold and silver, and then,
planting the huge anvil upon its block, he gripped
his mighty hammer in one hand, the other gripped his tongs.

And first Hephaestus makes a great and massive shield,
blazoning well-wrought emblems all across its surface,
raising a rim around it, glittering, triple-ply
with a silver shield-strap run from edge to edge
and five layers of metal to build the shield itself,

and across its vast expanse with all his craft and cunning
the god creates a world of gorgeous immortal work.

There he made the earth and there the sky and the sea
and the inexhaustible blazing sun and the moon rounding
     full
and there the constellations, all that crown the heavens,
the Pleiades and the Hyades, Orion in all his power too
and the Great Bear that mankind also calls the Wagon:
she wheels on her axis always fixed, watching Orion,
and she alone is denied a plunge in the Ocean's baths.

And he forged on the shield two noble cities filled
with mortal men. With weddings and wedding feasts in one
and under glowing torches they brought forth the brides
from the women's chambers, marching through the streets
while choir on choir the wedding song rose high
and the young men came dancing, whirling round in rings
and among them flutes and harps kept up their stirring
     call—
women rushed to the doors and each stood moved with won-
     der.
And the people massed, streaming into the marketplace
where a quarrel had broken out and two men struggled
over the blood-price for a kinsman just murdered.
One declaimed in public, vowing payment in full—
the other spurned him, he would not take a thing—
so both men pressed for a judge to cut the knot.

The crowd cheered on both, they took both sides,
but heralds held them back as the city elders sat
on polished stone benches, forming the sacred circle,
grasping in hand the staffs of clear-voiced heralds,
and each leapt to his feet to plead the case in turn.
Two bars of solid gold shone on the ground before them,
a prize for the judge who'd speak the straightest verdict.

But circling the other city camped a divided army
gleaming in battle-gear, and two plans split their ranks:
to plunder the city or share the riches with its people,
hoards the handsome citadel stored within its depths.
But the people were not surrendering, not at all.
They armed for a raid, hoping to break the siege—
loving wives and innocent children standing guard
on the ramparts, flanked by elders bent with age
as men marched out to war. Ares and Pallas led them,
both burnished gold, gold the attire they donned, and great,
magnificent in their armor—gods for all the world,
looming up in their brilliance, towering over troops.
And once they reached the perfect spot for attack,
a watering place where all the herds collected,
there they crouched, wrapped in glowing bronze.
Detached from the ranks, two scouts took up their posts,
the eyes of the army waiting to spot a convoy,
the enemy's flocks and crook-horned cattle coming . . .
Come they did, quickly, two shepherds behind them,
playing their hearts out on their pipes—treachery

never crossed their minds. But the soldiers saw them,
rushed them, cut off at a stroke the herds of oxen
and sleek sheep-flocks glistening silver-gray
and killed the herdsmen too. Now the besiegers,
soon as they heard the uproar burst from the cattle
as they debated, huddled in council, mounted at once
behind their racing teams, rode hard to the rescue,
arrived at once, and lining up for assault
both armies battled it out along the river banks—
they raked each other with hurtling bronze-tipped spears.
And Strife and Havoc plunged in the fight, and violent
    Death—
now seizing a man alive with fresh wounds, now one unhurt,
now hauling a dead man through the slaughter by the heels,
the cloak on her back stained red with human blood.
So they clashed and fought like living, breathing men
grappling each other's corpses, dragging off the dead.

  And he forged a fallow field, broad rich plowland
tilled for the third time, and across it crews of plowmen
wheeled their teams, driving them up and back and soon
as they'd reach the end-strip, moving into the turn,
a man would run up quickly
and hand them a cup of honeyed, mellow wine
as the crews would turn back down along the furrows,
pressing again to reach the end of the deep fallow field
and the earth churned black behind them, like earth churn-
    ing,

solid gold as it was—that was the wonder of Hephaestus'
work.

And he forged a king's estate where harvesters labored,
reaping the ripe grain, swinging their whetted scythes.
Some stalks fell in line with the reapers, row on row,
and others the sheaf-binders girded round with ropes,
three binders standing over the sheaves, behind them
boys gathering up the cut swaths, filling their arms,
supplying grain to the binders, endless bundles.
And there in the midst the king,
scepter in hand at the head of the reaping-rows,
stood tall in silence, rejoicing in his heart.
And off to the side, beneath a spreading oak,
the heralds were setting out the harvest feast,
they were dressing a great ox they had slaughtered,
while attendant women poured out barley, generous,
glistening handfuls strewn for the reapers' midday meal.

And he forged a thriving vineyard loaded with clusters,
bunches of lustrous grapes in gold, ripening deep purple
and climbing vines shot up on silver vine-poles.
And round it he cut a ditch in dark blue enamel
and round the ditch he staked a fence in tin.
And one lone footpath led toward the vineyard
and down it the pickers ran
whenever they went to strip the grapes at vintage—
girls and boys, their hearts leaping in innocence,

bearing away the sweet ripe fruit in wicker baskets.
And there among them a young boy plucked his lyre,
so clear it could break the heart with longing,
and what he sang was a dirge for the dying year,
lovely . . . his fine voice rising and falling low
as the rest followed, all together, frisking, singing,
shouting, their dancing footsteps beating out the time.

And he forged on the shield a herd of longhorn cattle,
working the bulls in beaten gold and tin, lowing loud
and rumbling out of the farmyard dung to pasture
along a rippling stream, along the swaying reeds.
And the golden drovers kept the herd in line,
four in all, with nine dogs at their heels,
their paws flickering quickly—a savage roar!—
a crashing attack—and a pair of ramping lions
had seized a bull from the cattle's front ranks—
he bellowed out as they dragged him off in agony.
Packs of dogs and the young herdsmen rushed to help
but the lions ripping open the hide of the huge bull
were gulping down the guts and the black pooling blood
while the herdsmen yelled the fast pack on—no use.
The hounds shrank from sinking teeth in the lions,
they balked, hunching close, barking, cringing away.

And the famous crippled Smith forged a meadow
deep in a shaded glen for shimmering flocks to graze,
with shepherds' steadings, well-roofed huts and sheepfolds.

And the crippled Smith brought all his art to bear
on a dancing circle, broad as the circle Daedalus
once laid out on Cnossos' spacious fields
for Ariadne the girl with lustrous hair.
Here young boys and girls, beauties courted
with costly gifts of oxen, danced and danced,
linking their arms, gripping each other's wrists.
And the girls wore robes of linen light and flowing,
the boys wore finespun tunics rubbed with a gloss of oil,
the girls were crowned with a bloom of fresh garlands,
the boys swung golden daggers hung on silver belts.
And now they would run in rings on their skilled feet,
nimbly, quick as a crouching potter spins his wheel,
palming it smoothly, giving it practice twirls
to see it run, and now they would run in rows,
in rows crisscrossing rows—rapturous dancing.
A breathless crowd stood round them struck with joy
and through them a pair of tumblers dashed and sprang,
whirling in leaping handsprings, leading out the dance.

And he forged the Ocean River's mighty power girdling
round the outmost rim of the welded indestructible shield.

And once the god had made that great and massive shield
he made Achilles a breastplate brighter than gleaming fire,
he made him a sturdy helmet to fit the fighter's temples,
beautiful, burnished work, and raised its golden crest
and made him greaves of flexing, pliant tin.

Now,
when the famous crippled Smith had finished off
that grand array of armor, lifting it in his arms
he laid it all at the feet of Achilles' mother Thetis—
and down she flashed like a hawk from snowy Mount Olym-
pus
bearing the brilliant gear, the god of fire's gift.

. . .

Book Twenty-Two
The Death of Hector

So all through Troy the men who had fled like panicked
      fawns
were wiping off their sweat, drinking away their thirst,
leaning along the city's massive ramparts now
while Achaean troops, sloping shields to shoulders,
closed against the walls. But there stood Hector,
shackled fast by his deadly fate, holding his ground,
exposed in front of Troy and the Scaean Gates.
And now Apollo turned to taunt Achilles:
"Why are you chasing *me*? Why waste your speed?—
son of Peleus, you a mortal and I a deathless god.
You still don't know that I am immortal, do you?—
straining to catch me in your fury! Have you forgotten?
There's a war to fight with the Trojans you stampeded,
look, they're packed inside their city walls, but you,
you've slipped away out here. You can't kill *me*—
I can never die—it's not my fate!"

                                    Enraged at that,
Achilles shouted in mid-stride, "You've blocked my way,
you distant, deadly Archer, deadliest god of all—
you made me swerve away from the rampart there.
Else what a mighty Trojan army had gnawed the dust

before they could ever straggle through their gates!
Now you've robbed me of great glory, saved their lives
with all your deathless ease. Nothing for you to fear,
no punishment to come. Oh I'd pay you back
if I only had the power at my command!"

No more words—he dashed toward the city,
heart racing for some great exploit, rushing on
like a champion stallion drawing a chariot full tilt,
sweeping across the plain in easy, tearing strides—
so Achilles hurtled on, driving legs and knees.

And old King Priam was first to see him coming,
surging over the plain, blazing like the star
that rears at harvest, flaming up in its brilliance,—
far outshining the countless stars in the night sky,
that star they call Orion's Dog—brightest of all
but a fatal sign emblazoned on the heavens,
it brings such killing fever down on wretched men.
So the bronze flared on his chest as on he raced—
and the old man moaned, flinging both hands high,
beating his head and groaning deep he called,
begging his dear son who stood before the gates,
unshakable, furious to fight Achilles to the death.
The old man cried, pitifully, hands reaching out to him,
"Oh Hector! Don't just stand there, don't, dear child,
waiting that man's attack—alone, cut off from friends!
You'll meet your doom at once, beaten down by Achilles,

so much stronger than you—that hard, headlong man.
Oh if only the gods loved him as much as I do . . .
dogs and vultures would eat his fallen corpse at once!—
with what a load of misery lifted from my spirit.
That man who robbed me of many sons, brave boys,
cutting them down or selling them off as slaves,
shipped to islands half the world away . . .
Even now there are two, Lycaon and Polydorus—
I cannot find them among the soldiers crowding Troy,
those sons Laothoë bore me, Laothoë queen of women.
But if they are still alive in the enemy's camp,
then we'll ransom them back with bronze and gold.
We have hoards inside the walls, the rich dowry
old and famous Altes presented with his daughter.
But if they're dead already, gone to the House of Death,
what grief to their mother's heart and mine—we gave them
    life.
For the rest of Troy, though, just a moment's grief
unless you too are battered down by Achilles.
Back, come back! Inside the walls, my boy!
Rescue the men of Troy and the Trojan women—
don't hand the great glory to Peleus' son,
bereft of your own sweet life yourself.

                              Pity me too!—
still in my senses, true, but a harrowed, broken man
marked out by doom—past the threshold of old age . . .
and Father Zeus will waste me with a hideous fate,
and after I've lived to look on so much horror!

62

My sons laid low, my daughters dragged away
and the treasure-chambers looted, helpless babies
hurled to the earth in the red barbarity of war . . .
my sons' wives hauled off by the Argives' bloody hands!
And I, I last of all—the dogs before my doors
will eat me raw, once some enemy brings me down
with his sharp bronze sword or spits me with a spear,
wrenching the life out of my body, yes, the very dogs
I bred in my own halls to share my table, guard my gates—
mad, rabid at heart they'll lap their master's blood
and loll before my doors.

> Ah for a young man
all looks fine and noble if he goes down in war,
hacked to pieces under a slashing bronze blade—
he lies there dead . . . but whatever death lays bare,
all wounds are marks of glory. When an old man's killed
and the dogs go at the gray head and the gray beard
and mutilate the genitals—that is the cruelest sight
in all our wretched lives!"

> So the old man groaned
and seizing his gray hair tore it out by the roots
but he could not shake the fixed resolve of Hector.
And his mother wailed now, standing beside Priam,
weeping freely, loosing her robes with one hand
and holding out her bare breast with the other,
her words pouring forth in a flight of grief and tears:
"Hector, my child! Look—have some respect for *this*!
Pity your mother too, if I ever gave you the breast

to soothe your troubles, remember it now, dear boy—
beat back that savage man from safe inside the walls!
Don't go forth, a champion pitted against him—
merciless, brutal man. If he kills you now,
how can I ever mourn you on your deathbed?—
dear branch in bloom, dear child I brought to birth!—
Neither I nor your wife, that warm, generous woman . . .
Now far beyond our reach, now by the Argive ships
the rushing dogs will tear you, bolt your flesh!"

So they wept, the two of them crying out
to their dear son, both pledging time and again
but they could not shake the fixed resolve of Hector,
No, he waited Achilles, coming on, gigantic in power.
As a snake in the hills, guarding his hole, awaits a man—
bloated with poison, deadly hatred seething inside him,
glances flashing fire as he coils round his lair . . .
so Hector, nursing his quenchless fury, gave no ground,
leaning his burnished shield against a jutting wall,
but harried still, he probed his own brave heart:
"No way out. If I slip inside the gates and walls,
Polydamas will be first to heap disgrace on me—
he was the one who urged me to lead our Trojans
back to Ilium just last night, the disastrous night
Achilles rose in arms like a god. But did I give way?
Not at all. And how much better it would have been!
Now my army's ruined, thanks to my own reckless pride,
I would die of shame to face the men of Troy

64

and the Trojan women trailing their long robes . . .
Someone less of a man than I will say, 'Our Hector—
staking all on his own strength, he destroyed his army!'
So they will mutter. So now, better by far for me
to stand up to Achilles, kill him, come home alive
or die at his hands in glory out before the walls.
But wait—what if I put down my studded shield
and heavy helmet, prop my spear on the rampart
and go forth, just as I am, to meet Achilles,
noble Prince Achilles . . .
why, I could promise to give back Helen, yes,
and all her treasures with her, all those riches
Paris once hauled home to Troy in the hollow ships—
and they were the cause of all our endless fighting—
Yes, yes, return it all to the sons of Atreus now
to haul away, and then, at the same time, divide
the rest with all the Argives, all the city holds,
and then I'd take an oath for the Trojan royal council
that we will hide nothing! Share and share alike the hoards
our handsome citadel stores within its depths and—
Why debate, my friend? Why thrash things out?
I must not go and implore him. He'll show no mercy,
no respect for me, my rights—he'll cut me down
straight off—stripped of defenses like a woman
once I have loosed the armor off my body.
No way to parley with that man—not now—
not from behind some oak or rock to whisper,
like a boy and a young girl, lovers' secrets

a boy and girl might whisper to each other . . .
Better to clash in battle, now, at once—
see which fighter Zeus awards the glory!"

So he wavered,
waiting there, but Achilles was closing on him now
like the god of war, the fighter's helmet flashing,
over his right shoulder shaking the Pelian ash spear,
that terror, and the bronze around his body flared
like a raging fire or the rising, blazing sun.
Hector looked up, saw him, started to tremble,
nerve gone, he could hold his ground no longer,
he left the gates behind and away he fled in fear—
and Achilles went for him, fast, sure of his speed
as the wild mountain hawk, the quickest thing on wings,
launching smoothly, swooping down on a cringing dove
and the dove flits out from under, the hawk screaming
over the quarry, plunging over and over, his fury
driving him down to beak and tear his kill—
so Achilles flew at him, breakneck on in fury
with Hector fleeing along the walls of Troy,
fast as his legs would go. On and on they raced,
passing the lookout point, passing the wild fig tree
tossed by the wind, always out from under the ramparts
down the wagon trail they careered until they reached
the clear running springs where whirling Scamander
rises up from its double wellsprings bubbling strong—
and one runs hot and the steam goes up around it,
drifting thick as if fire burned at its core

but the other even in summer gushes cold
as hail or freezing snow or water chilled to ice . . .
And here, close to the springs, lie washing-pools
scooped out in the hollow rocks and broad and smooth
where the wives of Troy and all their lovely daughters
would wash their glistening robes in the old days,
the days of peace before the sons of Achaea came . . .
Past these they raced, one escaping, one in pursuit
and the one who fled was great but the one pursuing
greater, even greater—their pace mounting in speed
since both men strove, not for a sacrificial beast
or oxhide trophy, prizes runners fight for, no,
they raced for the life of Hector breaker of horses.
Like powerful stallions sweeping round the post for trophies,
galloping full stretch with some fine prize at stake,
a tripod, say, or woman offered up at funeral games
for some brave hero fallen—so the two of them
whirled three times around the city of Priam,
sprinting at top speed while all the gods gazed down,
and the father of men and gods broke forth among them
    now:
"Unbearable—a man I love, hunted round his own city walls
and right before my eyes. My heart grieves for Hector.
Hector who burned so many oxen in my honor, rich cuts,
now on the rugged crests of Ida, now on Ilium's heights.
But now, look, brilliant Achilles courses him round
the city of Priam in all his savage, lethal speed.
Come, you immortals, think this through. Decide.

Either we pluck the man from death and save his life
or strike him down at last, here at Achilles' hands—
for all his fighting heart."

                           But immortal Athena,
her gray eyes wide, protested strongly: "Father!
Lord of the lightning, king of the black cloud,
what are you saying? A man, a mere mortal,
his doom sealed long ago? You'd set him free
from all the pains of death?

                                Do as you please—
but none of the deathless gods will ever praise you."

And Zeus who marshals the thunderheads replied,
"Courage, Athena, third-born of the gods, dear child.
Nothing I said was meant in earnest, trust me,
I mean you all the good will in the world. Go.
Do as your own impulse bids you. Hold back no more."

So he launched Athena already poised for action—
down the goddess swept from Olympus' craggy peaks.

And swift Achilles kept on coursing Hector, nonstop
as a hound in the mountains starts a fawn from its lair,
hunting him down the gorges, down the narrow glens
and the fawn goes to ground, hiding deep in brush
but the hound comes racing fast, nosing him out
until he lands his kill. So Hector could never throw
Achilles off his trail, the swift racer Achilles—

time and again he'd make a dash for the Dardan Gates,
trying to rush beneath the rock-built ramparts, hoping
men on the heights might save him, somehow, raining spears
but time and again Achilles would intercept him quickly,
heading him off, forcing him out across the plain
and always sprinting along the city side himself—
endless as in a dream . . .
when a man can't catch another fleeing on ahead
and he can never escape nor his rival overtake him—
so the one could never run the other down in his speed
nor the other spring away. And how could Hector have fled
the fates of death so long? How unless one last time,
one final time Apollo had swept in close beside him,
driving strength in his legs and knees to race the wind?
And brilliant Achilles shook his head at the armies,
never letting them hurl their sharp spears at Hector—
someone might snatch the glory, Achilles come in second.
But once they reached the springs for the fourth time,
then Father Zeus held out his sacred golden scales:
in them he placed two fates of death that lays men low—
one for Achilles, one for Hector breaker of horses—
and gripping the beam mid-haft the Father raised it high
and down went Hector's day of doom, dragging him down
to the strong House of Death—and god Apollo left him.
Athena rushed to Achilles, her bright eyes gleaming,
standing shoulder-to-shoulder, winging orders now:
"At last our hopes run high, my brilliant Achilles—
Father Zeus must love you—

we'll sweep great glory back to Achaea's fleet,
we'll kill this Hector, mad as he is for battle!
No way for him to escape us now, no longer—
not even if Phoebus the distant deadly Archer
goes through torments, pleading for Hector's life,
groveling over and over before our storming Father Zeus.
But you, you hold your ground and catch your breath
while I run Hector down and persuade the man
to fight you face-to-face."

               So Athena commanded
and he obeyed, rejoicing at heart—Achilles stopped,
leaning against his ashen spearshaft barbed in bronze.
And Athena left him there, caught up with Hector at once,
and taking the build and vibrant voice of Deiphobus
stood shoulder-to-shoulder with him, winging orders:
"Dear brother, how brutally swift Achilles hunts you—
coursing you round the city of Priam in all his lethal speed!
Come, let us stand our ground together—beat him back."

   "Deiphobus!"—Hector, his helmet flashing, called out to
     her—
"dearest of all my brothers, all these warring years,
of all the sons that Priam and Hecuba produced!
Now I'm determined to praise you all the more,
you who dared—seeing me in these straits—
to venture out from the walls, all for *my* sake,
while the others stay inside and cling to safety."

The goddess answered quickly, her eyes blazing.
"True, dear brother—how your father and mother both
implored me, time and again, clutching my knees,
and the comrades round me begging me to stay!
Such was the fear that broke them, man for man,
but the heart within me broke with grief for you.
Now headlong on and fight! No letup, no lance spared!
So now, now we'll *see* if Achilles kills us both
and hauls our bloody armor back to the beaked ships
or he goes down in pain beneath your spear."

Athena luring him on with all her immortal cunning—
and now, at last, as the two came closing for the kill
it was tall Hector, helmet flashing, who led off:
"No more running from you in fear, Achilles!
Not as before. Three times I fled around
the great city of Priam—I lacked courage then
to stand your onslaught. Now my spirit stirs me
to meet you face-to-face. Now kill or be killed!
Come, we'll swear to the gods, the highest witnesses—
the gods will oversee our binding pacts. I swear
I will never mutilate you—merciless as you are—
if Zeus allows me to last it out and tear your life away.
But once I've stripped your glorious armor, Achilles,
I will give your body back to your loyal comrades.
Swear you'll do the same."

A swift dark glance
and the headstrong runner answered, "Hector, stop!

You unforgiveable, you . . . don't talk to me of pacts.
There are no binding oaths between men and lions—
wolves and lambs can enjoy no meeting of the minds—
they are all bent on hating each other to the death.
So with you and me. No love between us. No truce
till one or the other falls and gluts with blood
Ares who hacks at men behind his rawhide shield.
Come, call up whatever courage you can muster.
Life or death—now prove yourself a spearman,
a daring man of war! No more escape for you—
Athena will kill you with my spear in just a moment.
Now you'll pay at a stroke for all my comrades' grief,
all you killed in the fury of your spear!"

       With that,
shaft poised, he hurled and his spear's long shadow flew
but seeing it coming glorious Hector ducked away,
crouching down, watching the bronze tip fly past
and stab the earth—but Athena snatched it up
and passed it back to Achilles
and Hector the gallant captain never saw her.
He sounded out a challenge to Peleus' princely son:
"You missed, look—the great godlike Achilles!
So you knew nothing at all from Zeus about my death—
and yet how sure you were! All bluff, cunning with words,
that's all you are—trying to make me fear you,
lose my nerve, forget my fighting strength.
Well, you'll never plant your lance in my back
as I flee *you* in fear—plunge it through my chest

as I come charging in, if a god gives you the chance!
But now it's for you to dodge *my* brazen spear—
I wish you'd bury it in your body to the hilt.
How much lighter the war would be for Trojans then
if you, their greatest scourge, were dead and gone!"

Shaft poised, he hurled and his spear's long shadow flew
and it struck Achilles' shield—a dead-center hit—
but off and away it glanced and Hector seethed,
his hurtling spear, his whole arm's power poured
in a wasted shot. He stood there, cast down . . .
he had no spear in reserve. So Hector shouted out
to Deiphobus bearing his white shield—with a ringing shout
he called for a heavy lance—

                              but the man was nowhere near him,
vanished—

            yes and Hector knew the truth in his heart
and the fighter cried aloud, "My time has come!
At last the gods have called me down to death.
I thought he was at my side, the hero Deiphobus—
he's safe inside the walls, Athena's tricked me blind.
And now death, grim death is looming up beside me,
no longer far away. No way to escape it now. This,
this was their pleasure after all, sealed long ago—
Zeus and the son of Zeus, the distant deadly Archer—
though often before now they rushed to my defense.
So now I meet my doom. Well let me die—
but not without struggle, not without glory, no,

in some great clash of arms, that even men to come
will hear of down the years!"

                          And on that resolve
he drew the whetted sword that hung at his side,
tempered, massive, and gathering all his force
he swooped like a soaring eagle
launching down from the dark clouds to earth
to snatch some helpless lamb or trembling hare.
So Hector swooped now, swinging his whetted sword
and Achilles charged too, bursting with rage, barbaric,
guarding his chest with the well-wrought blazoned shield,
head tossing his gleaming helmet, four horns strong
and the golden plumes shook that the god of fire
drove in bristling thick along its ridge.
Bright as that star amid the stars in the night sky,
star of the evening, brightest star that rides the heavens,
so fire flared from the sharp point of the spear Achilles
brandished high in his right hand, bent on Hector's death,
scanning his splendid body—where to pierce it best?
The rest of his flesh seemed all encased in armor,
burnished, brazen—*Achilles'* armor that Hector stripped
from strong Patroclus when he killed him—true,
but one spot lay exposed,
where collarbones lift the neckbone off the shoulders,
the open throat, where the end of life comes quickest—*there*
as Hector charged in fury brilliant Achilles drove his spear
and the point went stabbing clean through the tender neck
but the heavy bronze weapon failed to slash the windpipe—

Hector could still gasp out some words, some last reply ...
he crashed in the dust—

                      godlike Achilles gloried over him:
"Hector—surely you thought when you stripped Patroclus'
    armor
that you, you would be safe! Never a fear of me—
far from the fighting as I was—you fool!
Left behind there, down by the beaked ships
his great avenger waited, a greater man by far—
that man was I, and I smashed your strength! And you—
the dogs and birds will maul you, shame your corpse
while Achaeans bury my dear friend in glory!"

    Struggling for breath, Hector, his helmet flashing,
said, "I beg you, beg you by your life, your parents—
don't let the dogs devour me by the Argive ships!
Wait, take the princely ransom of bronze and gold,
the gifts my father and noble mother will give you—
but give my body to friends to carry home again,
so Trojan men and Trojan women can do me honor
with fitting rites of fire once I am dead."

    Staring grimly, the proud runner Achilles answered,
"Beg no more, you fawning dog—begging me by my parents!
Would to god my rage, my fury would drive me now
to hack your flesh away and eat you raw—
such agonies you have caused me! Ransom?
No man alive could keep the dog-packs off you,

not if they haul in ten, twenty times that ransom
and pile it here before me and promise fortunes more—
no, not even if Dardan Priam should offer to weigh out
your bulk in gold! Not even then will your noble mother
lay you on your deathbed, mourn the son she bore . . .
The dogs and birds will rend you—blood and bone!"

At the point of death, Hector, his helmet flashing,
said, "I know you well—I see my fate before me.
Never a chance that I could win you over . . .
Iron inside your chest, that heart of yours.
But now beware, or my curse will draw god's wrath
upon your head, that day when Paris and lord Apollo—
for all your fighting heart—destroy you at the Scaean
    Gates!"

Death cut him short. The end closed in around him.
Flying free of his limbs
his soul went winging down to the House of Death,
wailing his fate, leaving his manhood far behind,
his young and supple strength. But brilliant Achilles
taunted Hector's body, dead as he was, "Die, die!
For my own death, I'll meet it freely—whenever Zeus
and the other deathless gods would like to bring it on!"

With that he wrenched his bronze spear from the corpse,
laid it aside and ripped the bloody armor off the back.
And the other sons of Achaea, running up around him,

crowded closer, all of them gazing wonder-struck
at the build and marvelous, lithe beauty of Hector.
And not a man came forward who did not stab his body,
glancing toward a comrade, laughing: "Ah, look here—
how much softer he is to handle now, this Hector,
than when he gutted our ships with roaring fire!"

  Standing over him, so they'd gloat and stab his body.
But once he had stripped the corpse the proud runner Achil-
    les
took his stand in the midst of all the Argive troops
and urged them on with a flight of winging orders:
"Friends—lords of the Argives, O my captains!
Now that the gods have let me kill this man
who caused us agonies, loss on crushing loss—
more than the rest of all their men combined—
come, let us ring their walls in armor, test them,
see what recourse the Trojans still may have in mind.
Will they abandon the city heights with this man fallen?
Or brace for a last, dying stand though Hector's gone?
But wait—what am I saying? Why this deep debate?
Down by the ships a body lies unwept, unburied—
Patroclus . . . I will never forget him,
not as long as I'm still among the living
and my springing knees will lift and drive me on.
Though the dead forget their dead in the House of Death,
I will remember, even there, my dear companion.

                                              Now,

come, you sons of Achaea, raise a song of triumph!
Down to the ships we march and bear this corpse on high—
we have won ourselves great glory. We have brought
magnificent Hector down, that man the Trojans
glorified in their city like a god!"

                              So he triumphed
and now he was bent on outrage, on shaming noble Hector.
Piercing the tendons, ankle to heel behind both feet,
he knotted straps of rawhide through them both,
lashed them to his chariot, left the head to drag
and mounting the car, hoisting the famous arms aboard,
he whipped his team to a run and breakneck on they flew,
holding nothing back. And a thick cloud of dust rose up
from the man they dragged, his dark hair swirling round
that head so handsome once, all tumbled low in the dust—
since Zeus had given him over to his enemies now
to be defiled in the land of his own fathers.

So his whole head was dragged down in the dust.
And now his mother began to tear her hair . . .
she flung her shining veil to the ground and raised
a high, shattering scream, looking down at her son.
Pitifully his loving father groaned and round the king
his people cried with grief and wailing seized the city—
for all the world as if all Troy were torched and smoldering
down from the looming brows of the citadel to her roots.
Priam's people could hardly hold the old man back,
frantic, mad to go rushing out the Dardan Gates.

He begged them all, groveling in the filth,
crying out to them, calling each man by name,
"Let go, my friends! Much as you care for me,
let me hurry out of the city, make my way,
all on my own, to Achaea's waiting ships!
I must implore that terrible, violent man . . .
Perhaps—who knows?—he may respect my age,
may pity an old man. He has a father too,
as old as I am—Peleus sired him once,
Peleus reared him to be the scourge of Troy
but most of all to me—he made my life a hell.
So many sons he slaughtered, just coming into bloom . . .
but grieving for all the rest, one breaks my heart the most
and stabbing grief for him will take me down to Death—
my Hector—would to god he had perished in my arms!
Then his mother who bore him—oh so doomed,
she and I could glut ourselves with grief."

So the voice of the king rang out in tears,
the citizens wailed in answer, and noble Hecuba
led the wives of Troy in a throbbing chant of sorrow:
"O my child—my desolation! How can I go on living?
What agonies must I suffer now, now *you* are dead and
gone?
You were my pride throughout the city night and day—
a blessing to us all, the men and women of Troy:
throughout the city they saluted you like a god.

You, you were their greatest glory while you lived—
now death and fate have seized you, dragged you down!"

Her voice rang out in tears, but the wife of Hector
had not heard a thing. No messenger brought the truth
of how her husband made his stand outside the gates.
She was weaving at her loom, deep in the high halls,
working flowered braiding into a dark red folding robe.
And she called her well-kempt women through the house
to set a large three-legged cauldron over the fire
so Hector could have his steaming hot bath
when he came home from battle—poor woman,
she never dreamed how far he was from bathing,
struck down at Achilles' hands by blazing-eyed Athena.
But she heard the groans and wails of grief from the rampart
    now
and her body shook, her shuttle dropped to the ground,
she called out to her lovely waiting women. "Quickly—
two of you follow me—I must see what's happened.
That cry—that was Hector's honored mother I heard!
My heart's pounding, leaping up in my throat,
the knees beneath me paralyzed—Oh I know it . . .
something terrible's coming down on Priam's children.
Pray god the news will never reach my ears!
Yes but I dread it so—what if great Achilles
has cut my Hector off from the city, daring Hector,
and driven him out across the plain, and all alone?—
He may have put an end to that fatal headstrong pride

that always seized my Hector—never hanging back
with the main force of men, always charging ahead,
giving ground to no man in his fury!"

                                      So she cried,
dashing out of the royal halls like a madwoman,
her heart racing hard, her women close behind her.
But once she reached the tower where soldiers massed
she stopped on the rampart, looked down and saw it all—
saw him dragged before the city, stallions galloping,
dragging Hector back to Achaea's beaked warships—
ruthless work. The world went black as night
before her eyes, she fainted, falling backward,
gasping away her life breath . . .
She flung to the winds her glittering headdress,
the cap and the coronet, braided band and veil,
all the regalia golden Aphrodite gave her once,
the day that Hector, helmet aflash in sunlight,
led her home to Troy from her father's house
with countless wedding gifts to win her heart.
But crowding round her now her husband's sisters
and brothers' wives supported her in their midst,
and she, terrified, stunned to the point of death,
struggling for breath now and coming back to life,
burst out in grief among the Trojan women: "O Hector—
I am destroyed! Both born to the same fate after all!
You, you at Troy in the halls of King Priam—
I at Thebes, under the timberline of Placos,
Eetion's house . . . He raised me as a child,

that man of doom, his daughter just as doomed—
would to god he'd never fathered *me*!

                                    Now you go down
to the House of Death, the dark depths of the earth,
and leave me here to waste away in grief, a widow
lost in the royal halls—and the boy only a baby,
the son we bore together, you and I so doomed.
Hector, what help are you to him, now you are dead?—
what help is he to you? Think, even if he escapes
the wrenching horrors of war against the Argives,
pain and labor will plague him all his days to come.
Strangers will mark his lands off, stealing his estates.
The day that orphans a youngster cuts him off from friends.
And he hangs his head low, humiliated in every way . . .
his cheeks stained with tears, and pressed by hunger
the boy goes up to his father's old companions,
tugging at one man's cloak, another's tunic,
and some will pity him, true,
and one will give him a little cup to drink,
enough to wet his lips, not quench his thirst.
But then some bully with both his parents living
beats him from the banquet, fists and abuses flying:
'You, get out—you've got no father feasting with us here!'
And the boy, sobbing, trails home to his widowed mother . . .
Astyanax!

                    And years ago, propped on his father's knee,
he would only eat the marrow, the richest cuts of lamb,
and when sleep came on him and he had quit his play,

cradled warm in his nurse's arms he'd drowse off,
snug in a soft bed, his heart brimmed with joy.
Now what suffering, now he's lost his father—

Astyanax!

The Lord of the City, so the Trojans called him,
because it was you, Hector, you and you alone
who shielded the gates and the long walls of Troy.
But now by the beaked ships, far from your parents,
glistening worms will wriggle through your flesh,
once the dogs have had their fill of your naked corpse—
though we have such stores of clothing laid up in the halls,
fine things, a joy to the eye, the work of women's hands.
Now, by god, I'll burn them all, blazing to the skies!
No use to you now, they'll never shroud your body—
but they will be your glory
burned by the Trojan men and women in your honor!"

Her voice rang out in tears and the women wailed in answer.

PENGUIN 60s CLASSICS

READ MORE IN PENGUIN

For complete information about books available from Penguin and how to order them, please write to us at the appropriate address below. Please note that for copyright reasons the selection of books varies from country to country.

IN THE UNITED KINGDOM: Please write to *Dept. EP, Penguin Books Ltd, Bath Road, Harmondsworth, Middlesex* UB7 0DA.

IN THE UNITED STATES: Please write to *Consumer Sales, Penguin USA, P.O. Box 999, Dept. 17109, Bergenfield, New Jersey 07621-0120.* VISA and MasterCard holders call 1-800-253-6476 to order Penguin titles.

IN CANADA: Please write to *Penguin Books Canada Ltd, 10 Alcorn Avenue, Suite 300, Toronto, Ontario* M4V 3B2.

IN AUSTRALIA: Please write to *Penguin Books Australia Ltd, P.O. Box 257, Ringwood, Victoria 3134.*

IN NEW ZEALAND: Please write to *Penguin Books (NZ) Ltd, Private Bag 102902, North Shore Mail Centre, Auckland 10.*

IN INDIA: Please write to *Penguin Books India Pvt Ltd, 706 Eros Apartments, 56 Nehru Place, New Delhi 110 019.*

IN THE NETHERLANDS: Please write to *Penguin Books Netherlands bv, Postbus 3507, NL-1001 AH Amsterdam.*

IN GERMANY: Please write to *Penguin Books Deutschland GmbH, Metzlerstrasse 26, 60594 Frankfurt am Main.*

IN SPAIN: Please write to *Penguin Books S. A., Bravo Murillo 19, 1º B, 28015 Madrid.*

IN ITALY: Please write to *Penguin Italia s.r.l., Via Felice Casati 20, I-20124 Milano.*

IN FRANCE: Please write to *Penguin France S. A., 17 rue Lejeune, F-31000 Toulouse.*

IN JAPAN: Please write to *Penguin Books Japan, Ishikiribashi Building, 2-5-4, Suido, Bunkyo-ku, Tokyo 112.*

IN GREECE: Please write to *Penguin Hellas Ltd, Dimocritou 3, GR-106 71 Athens.*

IN SOUTH AFRICA: Please write to *Longman Penguin Southern Africa (Pty) Ltd, Private Bag X08, Bertsham 2013.*